GET SOME

Training in Common Sense

S. N Johnson

Cover design by S. N Johnson

Library of Congress Cataloging-in-Publication Data
Johnson, S. N
      Get Some: Training in Common Sense – 1st ed.
      ISBN 978-0-6151-5897-6

FIRST EDITION

Special Thank You to
Anne Basson
for her editing, guidance, and professionalism
in addition to Marty for their friendship.

Special Thank You to
Jovida Hill, Sharon Shields and Karen Gore
for their brainstorming the book's title with me.
Ladies that evening was fun. I can't wait to meet again.

This book is dedicated to my parents, their parents, a large network of aunts and uncles, and the family's friends that participated in raising me. Thank you for everything you took the time to teach, show and explain to me from the time of my memories and through our tomorrows.

Cheers to some of the strong women that continue to influence my life:

Roslyn Coleman: fresh rolls every Sunday, neighborhood guardian and Mom.
Peggy Gary: brothers are bigger, not their love, from you love is endless.
Mary Gilliam: outspoken and free, your class and frankness exuded spirit.
"Teacher" Janet Goldstein: teaching there is no shame in being intelligent.
Clara "Ruthie" Herring: proud and cleaver, showing beauty is how you feel.
Otellia "Stee" Holmes: the real survivor, you are the root I will never sever.
Delores Johnson: strong and quiet, you always displayed grace with intelligence.
Karen Johnson: not afraid to be heard above all the men, yet remaining elegant.
Shirley King: soft spoken and elegant, yet no pushover, duality you promote.
Bernadette Lloyd: an independent woman's hero, yet GOD and family first.
Beverly Lomax: everything natural and encouraging, you nourished me.
Mrs. Mary Perkins: forget the brand; we had our own who baked with love.
Grace Sullivan: perfectly named, always supporting the ones you love.
Josie Whitlock: for many years, bearing few and mothering many, you cared.
Nancy Wilson: songbird, strong, artistic, intelligent, loving, and optimistic.

...Never Least

My Mom: Ellen W. Johnson: "Hostess with the Mostest." You're my hero.

Being an invaluable friend means letting someone else talk while you actively listen.

S. N Johnson, 2006

"Every day is Christmas."

Said by Reverend Leon Sullivan, when asked why
he answered the phone 'Merry Christmas' in June.

The Machinist

S. N Johnson, 2006

Sew,
Threading through,
What seams,
Endless,
Side Stitches,
I run,
My life's color full quilt.

INTRO-DUCE-SING

Time and time again I am baffled by the lack of common sense and the failure to process train of thought that some people walk around displaying every day. Yes, I know, as one of my best friends repeats paraphrasing Voltaire whenever I get annoyed, "...common sense isn't common." Why not? Is it that hard to think? Among many other functions, the body thinks without much effort. As infants, we think with emotions and pictures until we discover how to formulate words. The brain processes while we sleep. We have little control over what is processed. Ever wake up from a deep sleep remembering something that was trying to be remembered all day? The brain does not stop. If we are not using common sense, we are fighting the brain's natural function to process. However, I have grown to understand an important factor and theory. Common sense is generated by the information previously endowed. Like computers need data to compute, data needs to be programmed into the brain to practice common sense. Without the information and training to produce the logic, common sense can not be realized. I offer within some points I have observed lacking in everyday life. To fill the void of training that I think has been lacking, I offer the theory: "Train and Explain:" More importantly, the practice of it.

For example, when the body decides it is time to go to the bathroom, it is time to go. Why we fight the urge and try to "hold" it has individual reasoning. Sometimes, due to a location, we can not go immediately. As a result, the body suffers cramps, pains, and worse: gas. To relieve the building pressure, the body might pollute the air of every nostril in its vicinity because it can not relieve itself properly. The family pet even moves away from the odor. Should we not cease to farting around and use the facilities? Is it difficult to wait and move out of everyone's airways before exploding? When I was a kid, my Mom every now and then would "expel gas" in the car during the Philadelphia winters. Get it: It was too cold to open a window and there was nowhere to run. My very proper mother would laugh at my reaction. I will never understand the desire to have other people smell the odorous incense of personal gastro developments nor how it adds to some individuals' pleasure. Is it not common sense that when relieving oneself for heaven's sake, take it outside? How about this: take it to the bathroom where disposal of waste matter and smells are expected and for the most part forgiven. One more thing, should the release arrive without warning, cease to walk around with it and stand still until it passes. No need to use human gas for propulsion or act like a hot air balloon.

As I am pleased to explain further: Before letting a gas expulsion escape, squeeze the buttocks cheeks together. Squeezing the buttocks checks is something that can be practiced anytime and anywhere without detection. Practice it when there is no need to "expel" gas. When the time comes, the muscles will be fit for the task. Beside not adding to the world's pollution an added benefit is a great "derriere" to show. Thus: this is an example of "Train and Explain."

My personal commitment to everyone who is lacking common sense is to share information and knowledge given to me that has provided me with the gift. In doing so, others will be able to reach the consciousness or non-consciousness of common sense. Those lacking will be transformed and their non-sleeping inner eyes opened to the logic.

Get Some – Training in Common Sense

I wonder how some people even get dressed. Then again, when seeing some of them, they are not successful in this either. Know what gets in my craw? Some of these people are affluent. They have beaucoup (that's French for too much) money. Possibly a reason they have lost the ability to think is that they have paid someone else to think and work for them. These people "manage." Manage to get up, manage to have bodily functions, and manage to shower, dress, and sometimes eat. Notice I did not say cook. No one cooks anymore. They have a chef cooking for them, stop on the way, or microwave. Challenged minds have stopped eating altogether and share the methods of their madness with others (i.e.: "Friends of A.N.A.") Sharing how not to eat is corrupting the process "train and explain" by people too insane to train. These corrupted trainers need to be trained by us: the sane. It's just common sense that the body needs food and healthy food to survive. Is it not?

Some with too much manage not to manage themselves. Worst yet, they raise children who do not think, work, nor manage. So we get inundated with more people who not only have no sense of being common, but walk around with a self-important attitude when they need to be kicked in the pride. Do not misunderstand; I have nothing against affluent people. I love the rich. I want them to love me back. Every girl dreams of her Prince Charming.

Get Some – Training in Common Sense

Yet, I once thought Diana was lucky until I understood her life with Prince Charles. Take note: my family and friends will not let anyone get away with murder with or without gloves, disappearing, coloring the hair in disguise. Scott Peterson believed in fiction. What was he thinking? He was thinking he could kill his wife and baby in order to start a new life. Neil Entwistle ran off to hide with his Mom and Dad in England after killing his wife and daughter in Massachusetts. Neither abused or murdered women nor their families should rest until justice is complete. To avoid the need, is it not common sense to file for divorce rather than commit a murder?

If I was a hotel empire millionaire's skinny blond daughter, instead of running around partying, getting drunk, being a groupie, dumping groupies, doing unreal reality shows, and appearing in supporting roles trying my best to not be an actress, I would be using Daddy's money and trying every career endeavor possible until I was happy with my own creation, my own name. I would exploit my name. I would manage my creation from the ground up and dominate the industry, so that people would respect me. I would do it several times until I got it right. Sure, I got started with Daddy's money; why not? I've got unlimited credit, but now I would be making my own and through intelligent methods. I would entertain because that is how I would network for more coverage.

I would give back to my fans and the communities that made me. I would eat! So bravo Paris, it is time to grow up and promote you. It does not matter if the media favors you. What matters is that you favor yourself. The more the press loves or hates you, the more your popularity. It is time to build positively on that popularity and ride your ride sober. It is time to learn from past poor decision making and turn yourself into the positive image that you can be proud of being. It is time to grow up.

Do not misunderstand; I have nothing against young wannabes not knowing what they "wanna be." Ha! I am an older "wannabe." Everyone has to find their way in his or her own way, time, and means. I should have been a trial lawyer. Should have been, but I was born under a stubborn rebels star and from there my parents should have known that I would do everything my way with their guidance. Once the chord was cut, it was all downhill with their control and uphill to my own mistakes. I loved making every one of those mistakes. My parents were always there catching me and throwing me back in the game. I am still in the game. I was never discouraged, except for moving into my father's apartment at the commencement of his newly separated marriage dating phase. Can not blame him; I was a "c-blocker" or sex blocker. Suffering from my own lack of common sense or denial, I did not realize he wanted to have sex with his younger girlfriend. It was never explained.

One of the young starlets I love to watch is Christina Aguilera. I hear some groans. Listen up. She has got lungs! She can belt out the notes live or in recordings. Some dislike Aguilera because she is sexy. Some think she dresses too sluttish. Some think Christina should stop hailing her sexuality. Guess what critics: Christina is laughing her way to Fort Knox. Forget about the bank. She could open her own branch and loan us money! In her time, some hated Marilyn Monroe for the same reasons. Marilyn stood over an air vent and let her dress blow up in the air almost showing her "coochie." This photo is renowned. When Sharon Stone spread her legs in "Basic Instinct," she was the talk of the drama. Now Britney not wearing underwear IS big drama. Ask most of your sisters, daughters, wives, and girlfriends if they always wear underwear. Do not be surprised of their responses. I know many men that do not wear them either. The real drama is that Britney did not know how to move in and out of a seated position while in a short skirt. That is where Britney needed some common sense etiquette training. Even if she was wearing underwear, the camera would have still shot an inappropriate photo. The photographer was still focusing in an inappropriate position by design or accident.

Get Some – Training in Common Sense

When I was a young girl, my next door neighbor's son, Douglas Coleman, would constantly remind me that I was a young lady. He was older and would tell me that young ladies sit with their legs closed. I was fortunate that I grew up with neighbors who cared and accepted the responsibility of other children in the neighborhood. Britney was apparently not as lucky. Oh, and let us not forget the always reinventing Madonna. Once shunned, I have now seen grandmothers rock it out to "Like a Virgin." Did you think I would stop there? Some of those grandmothers are unmarried and in their early thirty's. Causing thoughts to pause as to being like a virgin. This is a subject that will be approached a little further in these pages.

Still, there are some things that annoy the heck out of me. I want to voice them. The computer keys are mightier than the sword. I do not think that I am the only one annoyed by these habits. These are the little things that get discussed in bitch sessions. Many straight men may not understand what these sessions entail, but they should. On the other hand, my gay friends probably know. Having these sessions, does not define a gay man. However describing oneself as being on the "down low" is denying self and sexuality. Get on the seat and pee like us girls. No one is fooled. Being gay is not only an act of receiving anal sex. Take off those blinders and reach the common sense conclusion.

This book is my bitch session to the world. There is no common sense organization to my book. There are no short cuts to chapters as there are none to life. Each chapter is named to promote thought and amusement. I hope that everyone reading will think and be amused. The more amused thinking we do can help promote change and growth instead of ignorance.

You ask, "How?"
"Train and Explain"

Get Some – Training in Common Sense

RAIS'N CHILDREN WINE

Many often blame parents for many their shortfalls. How often do we thank our parents for what they did correctly? They were not wrong all the time. Even if most of the time they misjudged, we would not be able to continue living every day if their mistakes had not motivated us in some direction. Even should the motivation come from not wanting to be like them, and not wanting to duplicate their errors, we have learned.

Our parents and guardians have played an unavoidable influence on who we are today. It was not only them; it was and is every adult that we came in contact with either in person to person interaction or modern media. It

Get Some – Training in Common Sense

would only be reasonable to deduce what influences our own action will have on the world's youth. Adults are responsible for all the youth of the world. Former profession basketball athlete, Charles Barkley, could repeatedly be heard saying that he did not want to be a role-model. Once Charles Barkley decided to become a professional athlete, he decided to be a role-model. He was one whether he wanted to be or not like the role-models before him that influenced him. Unfortunately, he often short-sheeted his young fans of a needed leader. Despite Barkley's short-comings, it is the adults in the immediate influence of children that do have the choice and responsibility to explain who the good role-models are and who are not. It is the responsible adults that must steer the youths toward the proper and positive role-models. Many youth in the media carry a heavy responsibility for the other youth of the world. We raise tomorrow's idols, leaders, idiots, and killers. I would like to eliminate as much as possible the last two.

In our every day lives, we need to set the example. Years ago, I visited Germany. Even if no cars were approaching, the pedestrians waited for the traffic light that allowed them to walk across the street. At first, my American brain said, "Stop, Look both ways, Look again" and if it is safe to walk….WALK. My German friend explained that Germans felt it was their duty to set

20

examples for the children to wait for the light. It saved lives and taught them the importance of obeying rules. This following is an example of one German idealist. It also eludes common sense. Yet, with common sense logic, there must be some rules and morality to follow.

I am not going to be overly moral: moderately moral maybe, but not overly. Few can argue against theories that children learn and pick up from their surroundings. Many factors contribute to what they will and will not accept to display in their own behavior. I do not smoke. No one in my immediate family smokes. I drink occasionally. My parents and friends that visited our home drank occasionally. In my childhood memories, I have no recollection of anyone leaving our home drunk. Drugs were a "no brainer": do not do them, never thought of doing them, and knew that it would never be accepted by the adults that supervised me. I was obeying the rules while using common sense. I have never even seen cocaine, heroine, ecstasy, nor anything like them except through the media. Any inkling drugs were about to be used in my presence was a clue that it was time for me to leave. I did, still do, and will continue to do. For me, that was the common sense training I received. My parents never said "don't do drugs." I knew better. I honestly get high from life and my family's cheesecake.

What do adults that surround youthful eyes contribute? They contribute everything. When you are a happy person, children want to be around you. Children love to play and have fun. Children can not have fun around people who do not enjoy their laughter and the shrill of glee-filled screams. As adults, we explain and teach children where it is acceptable to play. Thus the phrases, "inside voice" and "outside voice" that we have heard uttered from our mouths or others. Enjoy and receive gaiety glee from a child that is laughing, playing, and screaming with joy on the playground, by the pools, even in the home's playroom or designated space for play and fun. Curtail and control the running, screaming, playing in the improper places such as the reception of a hotel, any restaurant, or travel venues: cars, planes, trains, and spaceships with the exception of places such as Chuck E Cheese. Thus, when we, the adults, need quiet time because we are doing something such as our taxes, explain the importance of the need for quiet and concentration ahead of time. Through the act of an understood explanation, we can avoid losing our patience with the child who does not understand the concentration and stress involved in preparing taxes and just wants to and needs to play.

Raising children means training children. Do not laugh. It is not in comparison with training the family pet. We train children's brains to understand and to process ideas, thoughts, and concepts. From the womb children are aware of another dimension. When they emerge, they are eager to develop and evolve. As infants, children work hard on communicating to adults what they need and want. In their own way, they train parents to understand their needs and wants. Children are steered by their observation and mimicking skills. When they learn to speak verbally and non-verbally, these skills do not cease. Children will constantly test and experiment on their boundaries. Training is what builds and molds the tools we give our children: our students. Training implies that we prepare the subject to be knowledge reinforced and successful in what they are trained. Motivation to use their training and progress comes from the tools they have received and the benefits reaped. While training, explanations in why the result is important and beneficial for all reinforce the development.

What are the goals of training our youth to smoke cigarettes, develop lung cancer, suffer agonizing pain, and die early? What are the goals of training our youth to drink excessively, get in a car, and commit suicide or murder? What are the goals of training our youth to do drugs, sell drugs, and/or prostitute their bodies? What are the goals of training our youth to cheat, steal, or murder? Someone please explain what is the goal in training our youth to have children out of wedlock, have children when they are still children, or not practice/have knowledge of safe sex? Where is the positive benefit? Can it be acceptably explained?

We must raise our children to produce positive results and appreciate the positive benefits. It is not only for their benefit, but for the benefit of all. We must train them to read, to write, to spell without spell check, and to count without the aid of fingers or calculators. We must train them to add, subtract, and to count without their fingers. We must train them to recognize danger and avoid it when possible. We must train them to look out for their fellow man. We must train them to think. We must train them to think for themselves. They need to learn how to process thought, and logic beyond mathematical equations:

Do not put your hand on the fire.
Fire is extremely hot.
Fire burns.
Burning destroys.
Burning hurts.
See this piece of leather.
The piece of leather is like the skin on your hand.
See what happens when I put the leather on the fire.
It burns

Get Some – Training in Common Sense

It sizzles.
If you put your hand on the fire, it will burn your hand.
Your hand will sizzle.
Your hand will hurt.
When you get hurt, you feel bad.
You cry.
Do you like it when you get hurt and cry?
Do not put your hand on the fire.
The adult must train and explain why.
It is not a quick nor easy process.
The child/student can be motivated not to want to feel pain if they understand that pain is unpleasant.
Subsequently, the next explanation is much easier:
Children should not play with matches.
Matches make fire.
The children will habitually process thoughts and concepts automatically because we have trained them how to process thoughts and concepts:

> *Matches can burn my hand.*

That is part of raising children.
Even now when I light a match, in the back of my mind I hear, "Be careful not to burn yourself." It is a cycle never to be broken. It is everyone's position in life and in the development of our culture: Train and Explain.

BONUS COMMON SENSE THOUGHT PROCESS:

• Getting pregnant by plan or otherwise means having a child, unless the fetus is aborted.

• Having a child and keeping the child means accepting responsibility for him or her.

• Accepting responsibility for a child means that child's life is your life all the time.

• Therefore, you become a parent.

• A part of being a responsible parent means that you can not leave children in unattended cars or alone in unsupervised homes, no matter what <u>you</u> need or want to do.

• Being a parent means *"it* is no longer all about you."

• A home is a safe environment that the parent or parents provide for children to grow and learn to become responsible adults.

• Being a responsible adult is not having children before you are prepared to become a parent caring for the child and providing a home for the rest of your or their life.

Get Some – Training in Common Sense

YOU NO AIN'T WHAT YOU ATE

Our health and well being has paramount importance to how we interact with each other and ourselves. If we eat healthy and feed our bodies, we feed our minds. When I was a very young girl in Catholic school, I often fell asleep in class in the mornings. One nun would take me to the coat room and tell me to eat something from my lunch. I did not understand why she wanted me to eat from my lunch. Nuns did not explain. They preached blind faith, and I was not about to ask. I thought it made the Sister happy, so I was glad to eat. Eventually, my mother, who was advised or retrained by the nun, explained to me that it was very important for me to eat breakfast every day. Breakfast gave me energy. Through receiving morning nourishment, I would not fall asleep in class. I have never forgotten that lesson. I have never understood people who do not want to eat. Energy expended needs energy consumed.

I grew up with food allergies. It was easier to list what I could eat than list what I could not. It was explained to me what would happen if I ate the foods that caused allergic reactions. I was trained to recognize these foods by experiencing what happened when I decided to ignore the explanations. My diet became substituted with foods high in carbohydrates. Being American, I also was raised around the notion of bigger is better. No one told me when I was a child that I was overeating. Eight pieces of toast with butter and grape jelly was normal to me. When my mother prepared pancakes or waffles for me, I was special. I was trained for comfort food. No one trained me on food groups and balanced meals. I never heard about portion control until after I was thirty. How to measure correct portion ratios of vegetables, carbohydrates, and proteins came from sources such as Weight Watchers and Oprah. Thinking Europeans ate too little, I soon learned Americans ate too much.

As a child, I ran, jumped rope, climbed hills, ice skated, hopped and skipped. I never knew I was exercising. I was having fun. Who renamed my fun activities as exercise? Exercise is not fun. How the food I consumed related to the energy I expended was never explained. It was not until Weight Watchers and Oprah that I understood the results of one exceeding the other. Who renamed my having a complete diet to having to go on a diet? Constantly allowing and supplying pizza, franchise menus, fried, trans-fat saturated, and high in calories foods train our students: the children, in unhealthy habits. Explaining how foods work and teaching our students to recognize how to eat and when to stop eating is training good habits. First, some of us need to be retrained. I, too, continue trying.

Parents are the guardians that care for the health and well being of children. Yet, they often do not explain to the children "the why." That is the reason children are repeatedly asking "why." As a result, grown-ups do not understand why they need to take care of their health. They do not understand why it is important to have preventative check-ups. When we are children, our parents are responsible for ensuring that check-ups are performed. Even the parents receive reminder notifications from the family's physicians. The child is just transported.

Many parents have let the schools teach their children some of the essential details of health. I learned sex education in school. I first saw a condom in and out of its packaging in school. I first touched a slimy condom in a classroom setting in school. The first time the gay culture was explained to me was in school. The function of the penis and what it looked like was explained in school. By the time my parents decided to discuss sex with me, I had read about it and asked my questions of the teachers. Mind you, I was lucky. At least someone taught me the facts. My eldest sister thought she was protecting me when she told me that I could get pregnant if a boy released his sperm in the swimming pool and it got into my bathing suit. She thought she was protecting me when she told me that sperm could travel from a boy's penis through the zipper in his pants and through my clothing. My sister explained that I should be careful not to slow dance with boys because I could get pregnant. She believed she was sheltering me when she told me that if a boy had "touched himself" and afterwards touched a doorknob, should I touch the same door knob that I could get pregnant. Imagine how long I did not touch doorknobs with my bare hands. Thank goodness for teachers.

If we do not spread the knowledge and explain the train of thought behind the knowledge, how could we possibly expect children to understand the common sense behind certain processes? How could children who will later become adults understand why abstinence, birth control, and/or safe sex are important and life altering decisions unless we explain?

In order to watch our health, we must monitor what we put in our bodies in every orifice of our bodies. We must exercise our minds and bodies. If we put more energy in and expend less energy, the body will become unfit. Putting in the wrong energy, is like putting Johnson's Body Oil into a car's engine, the inner workings of its body will breakdown. More so, the mind and body will not function correctly.

At the core of good health is a healthy mind. Trainers who are negative, abusive, or even absent can not nurture. These types of trainers collapse the personality and good nature of their subjects. Negative trainers or negative parents break down growing minds instead of building them. Thus their subjects or children develop unhealthy minds. They develop unhealthy habits. More poignant is they become copies of their mentors. The bad training begets bad trainers, and so on.

By setting the examples and explaining the reasons, we empower. While looking after our own health, we teach the foundations of looking after the self. We may not want to be an example, but by consciously agreeing to remain in this world, we are one. It is a lot of responsibility. While continuing to develop our mind, we train others to continue developing theirs "until death do us part."

BONUS COMMON SENSE THOUGHT PROCESS:

• Eating well helps promote good health, fit minds and bodies.

• Occasionally, lack of time and preparation prevent diners from eating well.

• By choosing foods simple and fast, diners often opt for fast food chains for themselves and their children.

• Some choices from fast food chains are unhealthy and promote obesity.

• Relying on these chains too frequently can promote bad eating habits.

• Bad eating habits do not promote good health nor fit mind and bodies.

Get Some – Training in Common Sense

CLEN-THEE-NEST

While working in a resort in the Bahamas, I met an intelligent girl who wanted to be a screenwriter. She had many great ideas, and she was ambitious. There was something very wrong or just "not right." She was dirty, very dirty. Her fair Caucasian complexion often would appear gray to the point that it was obvious when she would finally decide to bathe. She rarely washed her clothes. The white sweater that she constantly wore became a dirty light gray sweater. She would have safe sex, and sleep with the condom on or under her pillow for a week...which was hygienically unsafe. The resort's housekeepers refused to clean her room because they could not negotiate around the clothes and clutter and were disgusted by the filth in the room. This could not be something she decided to do when she started working at the resort. This is something she was allowed to do long before. This was a result of lack of training, and the lack of understanding the importance of one's hygiene and image.

After experiencing disgust, what is the first thought about someone with bad teeth? Maybe it is that they were not taught any better. What is the thought when seeing someone with beautiful teeth? They have a great dentist and adopted good habits. That is unless you see them flossing or picking their teeth at the table, in the office, or in a car. All in one glance, we can see the benefits of a nice smile versus a bad one. All in one glance, we make a judgment.

Teaching cleanliness is a form of example setting. The degree of cleanliness is adapted by the subject. My mother is a firm believer and practices "planning clothes for the week." My mother also would put the clothes she would wear the next day "out" the night before. This is a training that I rejected. I still stand in the closet and glare at the clothes trying to decide what fits my mood. However, I hang up my clothes, put them in the hamper, and sort them to wash. A training that I will never forget was that while I was watching TV on a Saturday afternoon, my mother told me to do my laundry. I told her that I did not want to miss the program. She simply told me to put it in the washer machine and dryer during the commercials. When it was time to fold, I could do it while still watching the programs. As sad as it is to admit that I was a TV zombie, it did instill at an early age something called: time management. Time management has proved invaluable to me. It also taught me the quicker I took my clothes out of the dryer, the fewer clothes I had to iron. This logic led to my motivation.

Another form of training I will never forget is that we were not allowed to leave dishes in the kitchen sink. Nor were we allowed to do anything until the kitchen was cleaned. My mother would wake us out of a sound sleep to clean our dishes. Save any expressed pity for our being awakened, we only had to rinse and place the dishes in one of two dishwashers. You read correctly, we had two. We were not unfortunate nor were we "washing dishes." More so, we were quickly trained not to be lazy even with the possession of these modern machines. This was a lesson and training we soon heeded because we liked uninterrupted sleep. If we wanted to sleep or enjoy free time, we learned to do our chores properly and before my mother returned home. My mother would leave us a list of chores to do while she was out of the house. So not to be confused, each daughter had her own list of chores. My very wise mother would call us one hour before her return home. The phone call was an announcement to get the chores finished before she arrived. We did. Now as an adult, I have adopted the habit of taking care of business first and having fun afterwards. I have also adopted the habit of making lists and checking off each task's completion. Not only does it make the fun more rewarding and less stressful, but the fun does not get interrupted.

LITTERING

I appreciate beautiful flowers and green parks. I love long walks and smelling fresh air. Nothing irritates me more than people who dump their waste on the ground. What makes me more irate is people who throw trash next to trash cans or put empty soda cans on top of trash cans instead of in them. If the throw misses the trash can, bend over and pick it up and *put the trash in a trash can.* If the trash can is too full, use a different receptacle or bound up the trash and put in another trash liner. This all depends on the locale and responsibility. The results of overflowing trashcans exemplify no thought or logic other than laziness. For those that feel the need to throw trash and cigarettes out of the window of cars, be assured that there is a trash receptacle at 99.9% of drivers' destinations. Instead of polluting, one should hold disposals until reaching one's destination.

In just about everyone's experience is the frustration of finding chewing gum in the most annoying places. Not only is the manner in which some people dispose of their used breath-freshening, teeth-whitening gum annoying, but it is unhygienic.

Thus some instant training and suggestions: keep the wrapper to encase used gum and dispose of both in trash receptacles. Train and explain why we do not spit gum out anywhere nor stick it under tables, under seats, nor on walls…unless the TV character MacGyver is doing something magical. Improperly disposed of gum ruins shoes, clothes, furniture, carpet, and spread germs. In some countries like Singapore, the government has intervened by prohibiting the sale and possession of chewing gum. Singapore is a very clean place, so leave the chewing gum at home. In Singapore, the law is very clear and very serious even for chewing gum.

CIGARETTES

Disposal of cigarettes run the same gamut. This is a habit that one consciously decides to adopt. If the smell of ashes and smelling like smoke repulses, reconsider the habit. Do not throw cigarettes out of car windows. Do not throw cigarettes on any floor or ground. The ability to flick cigarette butts in the air and into the bushes amazes few. Ashes go in the ashtrays and not on our green earth. The most irking is some scuba divers who smoke. They marvel at the inhabitants of the sea and the beauty within only to surface, smoke a cigarette and throw it into the waters. At which I will usually comment that I did not recall seeing any fish "bumming" a cigarette.

Ever been on the beach, enjoying the fresh sea air and cigarette smoke drifts into your nostrils? I am completely in favor of smoking and non-smoking sections everywhere.

I hold the responsible smokers, please forgive the oxymoron, responsible for the offensive smokers who exhibit poor smoking habits. If smoking is a must, smoke responsibly, train, and educate peers on what is acceptable so that they can smoke responsibly as well.

BONUS COMMON SENSE THOUGHT PROCESS:

• There are outer clothing and under garments.

• Under garments are in direct contact with the body and bodily fluids.

• Clothes that are in contact with bodily fluids become dirty after one wear even a brief wear. (pun intended)

• The habit of recycling undergarments without first washing them is dirty.

• If you are going to wear underwear, do not wear dirty undergarments.

Get Some – Training in Common Sense

SEX
(Calling it what it is!)

Other than the knowledge shared by my protective sister, I grew up with a healthy attitude towards sex. My parents did make books available for me. I do not know if they did this consciously, but they encouraged reading. The books that expounded on intercourse and sexual experimentation were on the bookshelves in our home library. Parents who fear the books that children are exposed forget their role as parents. Similar to the discussion of drugs, the information in books whether it be the bible or books about gay relationships needs a parental follow-up, guidance, and input. Do not censor the books, educate the child.

I remember going to a Sidney Sheldon book-adapted movie with my parents. During the film, there was not only complete nudity, but explicit sex scenes. There was a rape scene and a scene were a girl used ice cubes around a man's genitalia. I remember both my parents gazing expectedly at me. With my peripheral vision, I saw their heads turn to observe me. I was dedicated not to show my shock or embarrassment. On the contrary of some believers, I did not want to go out and have sex after seeing the movie. Nor did I think of ice cubes other than something to cool drinks. It was just more information for my knowledge bank. With the information and explanations that I already possessed combined with what I had seen in the movie, I could logically make decisions when it was time for me to experience that other dimension of adult life. I would make a withdrawal from that information bank much later in life. I never forgot what tricks they did in that movie or how much the guy in the movie was enjoying them.

HAVING SEX versus MAKING LOVE

It is not the same.
There is a time for one and a time for the other.
Some partners are for one and some partners for the other. If lucky, one partner who is great for both is

optimum. Otherwise, a decision is reached which is more apt in one's committed relationship. If wise, help a partner recognize when one, as opposed to the other, is desired. In the meantime, communicating to him or her how to keep the magic pleasing and interesting will help maintain the relationship.

Show this section to mates, and train them. Leave the book conveniently open to this section, or copy the page and post it on the refrigerator door or back of the toilet seat. These notions are definitely not taught by most of our parents nor teachers. We learn them from our friends who learn them from other friends. Before "Sex and the City," many women would not have dared to utter the words "fuck buddy," out loud except to a very close friend. Now, many women have emerged unabashed of their sexuality because of a TV series. Such training can be considered morally backwards or developed sexual awareness depending on your point of view. Continued training in this depends on personal and moral beliefs.

BIRTH CONTROL vs. ABSTINENCE

I do not want to speak morally on behalf of others' beliefs. I do not want to talk about pro-life or the right to choose. I only want to say that we must educate. We must inform the youth to make intelligent decisions. We must prepare them and show them why or why not. We must explain that having a baby is for life, every second and every minute of all lives intertwined. We must explain to them the responsibility and how they must bear the responsibility. We must help them realize that the desire to be needed and loved, the desire to "hang on" to a man, and the need for more financial support is not fulfilled through giving birth. Giving birth is a woman's passage to committed nourishing and not being nourished. We must encourage maturity, adopting a cat, bringing up a dog, or getting another job if the end need is anything other than the desire to nurture another human being. We must explain that every act of unprotected sex means not only the possibility of pregnancy, but carries the possibility of transmitting incurable diseases one of which may result in death.

BONUS COMMON SENSE THOUGHT PROCESS:

• Abstinence: the only non-surgical birth control 100 percent effective: no pregnancy or sexually transmitted diseases.

• Deciding to participate in sexual activities is a decision that must be made by a mature person with supporting information as well as parental, professional, medical, and educational advice.

• Becoming sexually active before reaching maturity and without the above-mentioned advice will lead to an area of emotional and physical vulnerability that can result in erroneous choices.

• These erroneous choices can lead to the belief in life-altering sweet temptations whispered with charm and romance such as: "It won't hurt" "You can't get pregnant the first time" "If I pull out beforehand, you won't get pregnant" "I don't like condoms, and anyway you are the only one" "I don't have any diseases" "If you do this for me, it means that you love me" "It is your duty" "You can make money to get you through. I will protect you."

• If there is a desire to believe those charming phrases, Stop and Run away do not walk. The proper level of maturity for engaging in intercourse has not been reached.

Get Some – Training in Common Sense

FRESH DRESSING

The way we dress reflects our character. Dressing also reflects our mood and the way we want to present ourselves. One day when I was lounging around the house in sweats, my mother asked me, her seventeen-year-old rebel daughter, to go and "dress pretty for her." I adorned what I thought would be a sluttish style to enforce my rebel teenage mind. I wore a hot red silk blouse unbuttoned to an ample cleavage, tight blue jeans, high red pumps, made up my face including hot red lipstick with an abundance of gloss, and adorned my hair with a big red bow. That fated day, an older boy came to the house with family friends who I would eventually relinquish my virginity to on the eve of my eighteenth birthday. It was bound to happen, but I still wonder if it would have been him if I had stayed in my sweats. Parents, peers, magazines, fashion shows, and even finances train the mind how to dress.

USE A FULL LENGTH MIRROR
and A TRUE FRIEND

Only the mirrors in the carnivals distort images. It is always evident that person who did not check the mirror before they walked out of the door. It was either that or they forgot to wear their glasses when looking. There is nothing more valuable than the friend or relative that says, "Are you going to wear that?" Keep this friend close because they are truer than true.

Mind, not many are guiltier of forgetting this rule than me. I own "fat clothes" and "thin clothes." There is nothing in my closet that is my "in between clothes." In between is where I spend most of my time. Being that I am endowed with a huge rear trunk, you would think that I would learn to turn around and check out not only what people will see coming but also what they will see going. Even I am in the process of being retrained.

OLD PEOPLE IN YOUNG CLOTHES

If you have got the body, the looks, and the attitude, go for it. Anyone who tells you differently is jealous of what you have. I have nothing else to say.

YOUNG PEOPLE IN OLD PEOPLES CLOTHES

When I was a little girl, I would see a pretty dress or pretty outfit and want it. My mother and sometimes both parents always took me shopping. I vividly remember my mother telling me "That's too old for you." Have parents stopped saying this to children? Was it just my mom? Why today with pedophiles roaming everywhere and baiting children on the Internet would a parent let their five-year-old daughter wear pants with "Tasty" or "Juicy" written across the buttocks? Can I get an AMEN? I am sending out a Bulletin, because some did not get the Memo: Just because the manufacturers make it, the stores sell it, and you think it is cute, does not mean it has to be bought. I hear the skeptics out there. "Just because I dress this way, does not invite someone to rape me." In many ways, this is absolutely correct, but why put out the invitation? While getting everyone's attention to the rear extremity, the derelict's attention was in the same crowd. I have a thought: If we let companies use our buttocks like a billboard, they should pay us for the advertisement space. The bigger the rear means the more advertisement space for rent. We should profit from our assets.

FLIP FLOPS AND SLIDES

The most obnoxious footwear and sound coming from footwear that anyone could put on bare feet. First, I know the attraction of these semi-feet coverings, especially when going to the beach. However, does one have to make that sliding sound as one walks? Walking is a motion of heel to toe and not heel, heel, heel. What is more annoying than persons who do not pick up their feet and slide their shoes across the floor? Cavemen even walked better. If I was to slide my feet across the floor as a child, an aunt's heavy hand would slap across the back of my head with the words "pick up your feet" to follow. The first slap hurts enough to remember what not to do to get the second or third. Logic learned from the fire analogy. If it hurt without pleasure, I do not need to repeat it. Funny thing, most people don't slide their bare feet.

EXPOSED TOES

Scrub them, clean them, paint them and if we can not make them pretty, cover them. Gentlemen can have nice feet, too.

Do not trim toes with teeth. Do not even put feet and the mouth in contact with the other. It is not acceptable. It is not hygienic. There are tools created for it. Refer to the section on cleanliness.

BONUS COMMON SENSE THOUGHT PROCESS:

• Hang up and fold your clothes and they will not wrinkle.

• Do not wear wrinkled clothing.

• Do not wear clothing that have holes in it unless they were bought that way and in fashion as absurd as it sounds.

• Learn to sew and iron or hire someone to do it for you.

• If you wear wrinkled and/or clothes with holes you appear sloppy, therefore not presentable.

• If you are not presentable, you will not be respected.

•If you do not want to be respected, you have wrinkles and holes in your head.

ADOPT A WORK HOBBIT

As a life trainer, preparing students for taking on their own responsibilities is an important goal. The logic used in training them to handle every day tasks is paramount in the way they will react to bigger and more important tasks later in life. All of this starts with organization. Organization is not the same for everyone. Some people's unorganized messes emerge with surprising order. Some people spend so much time putting things in order that they lose sight of the ultimate goal. As a child, my father would have me place his money flat, organize it by denominations, and have all the bills facing the same direction. As a manager, I used to hound a bank cashier who would not have his money all facing the same direction. It created tension in our work relationship.

What I thought was important, was not important to him. I awoke to a new understanding; his accounting work was consistently accurate. His financing balanced. The resort's safe was organized and secure. So why was I hounding him on what direction the heads on the bills were facing? I stopped. No more conflict. I was retrained.

Sometimes, results are the most important factor and not how the results are reached. Some people cook or bake and clean up afterwards. If they are a good cook, how the kitchen looks after the preparation is less important. How clean the kitchen was *before* they started cooking is extremely important. My father taught me how to bake. He also trained me to clean while I baked. He explained during sessions, that if we clean as we prepare, the item would be available when we were ready to use it later. This of course made sense, common sense once it was practiced. For instance, when making a cake, as the butter and sugar are being creamed in the mixer, the cup used to measure the sugar can be cleaned. Now, when the mixture is done creaming, the cup is ready for measuring the flour. Better yet, every element is measured ahead of time for quick and easy mixing. This is an optimum procedure when baking more than one item at the same time. Cooking shows often have everything pre-measured and that is why those kitchens are so neat and presentable.

Get Some – Training in Common Sense

I do not know many people who like to clean. I am one of those exceptions. I love cleaning. Not because of the act of cleaning, but the result. Cleaning while baking pleases me because the result is that everything is done. When the cake goes in the oven, the kitchen is clean. I can either start the next project, or relax. I have accomplished two tasks at once. That motivates me.

As a child, I was unknowingly to myself being trained in organization, time management, and multi-tasking. These skills became habit forming because of the benefits I enjoyed. I organized my schoolwork for what needed more time, more concentration, and/or more assistance. If there was an hour of reading that needed to be done, I did it in the library during class breaks or on the train ride home. As a result, when I arrived at home to do my schoolwork, I had less work to do.

Now, as an adult, I know how to organize my work. I know how to organize my day, week, and month. I know how to get important tasks done first and have fun later. I have learned how to get rid of the things I hate to do the most ahead of the others. I do not dread the finish because the hardest or most undesirable task is out of the way.

Get Some – Training in Common Sense

In management training seminars, I would sit in disbelief of what was being taught because my parents had taught me many of the concepts as a child. One of those lessons consisted of "how to talk to people during a conflict." The method of using the words "I felt …" instead of "You made me feel…" when confronting an abuser improves communication rather than closing it. Using the words, "could you," "would you," or "it would be helpful if" rather than "I need you to," will make the person being addressed less rebellious. At twenty-five years of age, some managers-in-training were hearing this for the first time; I had heard it before I was ten from my mother. I remember calling my mother, reporting about the training program, and thanking her for the training she gave me that others never learned and were having difficulties practicing.

So why are some employees not as productive as their potential? They have not been trained or not been trained correctly. What I learned easily at ten years of age is going to take a lot more convincing to someone who is twenty-five years old. It will also take a lot more patience. To reach departmental goals, employees need to exceed their potentials.

Employees must be trained to possess the skills to reach the goal. The importance of reaching the goal and how *together* the goal can be accomplished must be explained. How the employee will benefit is extremely important to each individual of the team. No one wants to do something for nothing. If there is a breakdown, retrain. If retraining the employees does not work, maybe the leader needs to be retrained. Often part of the training received is recognizing when the problem is not the training, but may be the trainer.

BONUS COMMON SENSE THOUGHT PROCESS:

• Through education from home and institutions, proper language skills and how to speak are taught.

• Speaking a language properly and using proper language skills presents an intelligent image.

    • Do not use words such as: hon', honey, sweetie, or dear when addressing people or customers.

        • Do not end sentences with prepositions such as: "where are you at?" or "that is where I went to." The sentences work without the last word: the preposition.

• Presenting an intelligent image will be an asset at the time of interviewing for professional positions.

• By interviewing for professional positions, a professional career can be achieved.

• Having a professional career, gives power over self.

• Being empowered can create survivors.

• Surviving is invaluable.

RELATIONBOATS
(Sex is a different vessel)

DATING

I will discuss dating and only dating because I know nothing about marriage, except what I have observed from the outside. Therefore, to say I know anything about marriage would be a farce. I, however, have a premise that marriage is dating for a longer period of time. I would say for life, though I have also learned and unfortunately been trained that some people do not marry for life. Some marry with an exit: defined as divorce in mind. In alignment, there are also some people who just are in love with the idea of being married: two, three, and more than four times. This type of marriage is disguised speed dating: maybe just an excuse to receive an abundance of gifts and have endless parties. Possibly they are trying to fill a round hole with a square peg.

When I was an early teenager, my mother admonished me for telephoning boys. She told me that young ladies do not call boys. She told me that proper young ladies wait for boys to call them. If I had listened to my mother and not been such a teenage rebel, I would probably still be a virgin. To this day, I am not sure if she was correct or not. I know, however, I have had more fun calling than waiting by the phone for a call.

Moms today do not only have to preach about who is initiating the calls; they have to monitor the Internet exchanges of their young girls and boys. They have to be concerned with what is being exchanged through the Web cameras. Today, the warning of calling a boy turns into the warning of chatting with a boy and exchanging photos or web camera shots. Or more severe, who their daughters may think is a boy, but turns out to be a grown man disguised as a boy with the sole purpose of fulfilling pedophile fantasies. Recently in the summer of 2006 news, it could be a government official or schoolteacher exchanging communications with our young ones.

Get Some – Training in Common Sense

Though the practice of dating has changed, it is also performed in the conventional ways. We still wait for our friends to introduce us to "their friends." We still hope to meet someone at a friend's wedding. We have tried to meet our matches through religious gatherings, fitness venues, sporting events, grocery shopping, bars, and nightclubs. To add to our attempts, we have turned desperate and publicized ourselves in the newspapers, on the Internet, on billboards, and televised dating programs.

By whatever means one can find true love, I am all for it. What to do with true love when found is where the training must enter. Preparing for love puts a spin on the emotion's spontaneity. Many women fall in love with men they choose to be intimated. Opening up our legs for entry is a gift given to someone perceived to be worthy. Deciding that someone is worthy is a form of caring for that person. Most men have learned that ultimately the decision to have sex is the decision of the woman. No matter how much spoken charm, gifts giving, and attention a man can give, if a woman does not want to open, the door will remain closed. Without diminishing its importance, sex should be the last detail to be discussed about dating.

Dating has lost its grace. It has evolved, correction, it has been transformed, into speed dating. I am not referring to the practice of going to a choreographed event where one meets as many potential mates within one hour while a whistle announces when it is time to move on to another conversation and another potential mate. I am referring to the act of trying to have as many dates as possible before deciding to commit. Sowing our oats and playing the field has become an act for both sexes, no matter the sexual preference. Some forget to stop dating others after marriage.

We need to slow down and smell…. We need to treat dating like the process of planting and pollinating flowers. We need to treat the preparation for dating like preparing the earth for planting. If the earth is not ready for the seeding, and in the beginning it is not, we need to turn the earth and toil it. Our minds and our hearts are the soil. When the soil is ready, we can introduce a plant or a seed. The plant or seed is our partner. Together the soil and the plant work together to grow or develop a third factor. This factor is a relationship. This factor is not yet a child. Passing autumns, winters, frost, being fertilized, trapping rainwater and feeding off the water shared between the soil and the plant are experiences. With the experiences shared together, the soil and the plant become inseparable, rooted and entwined together. If the relationship between them is strong, the plant and the soil can not survive without each other. There are some soils that are not correct or conducive to certain plants. If they are not correct for each other, one drains the life from the other. When the soil is correct, even if the plant is moved to another location, the soil around it has to travel, too.

Where does common sense enter? If the feeling of being drained of life or individuality in a relationship is present, maybe it is in the wrong soil. Together in a relationship, individual characteristics should be maintained like the soil will always be soil and the plant will always be a plant. Neither the plant nor the soil demands change from the other entity. They provide support to one another to promote growth or advancement. In a relationship, one does not train the other to be something other than the entity they were attracted. If training is need, it is done by a "farmer." The "farmer" that prepares the soil and does the planting is a minister, therapist, or counselor. They gather their knowledge to assist in the growth process of the relationship without assigning fault to either entity. Weeds grow without farming, but wheat grows with farming. Though both can be pretty to observe on the hill, only one can provide refined nourishment and growth.

The soil and the plant make something new that can nourish and grow. They can survive apart, but nothing emerges from their individuality. Even as the plant sheds leaves, it gives back protection and nutrients to the soil. Together they continue in their cycles and relationship and develop strong deep roots. A strong relationship must be rooted in trust, commitment, and friendship to weather oncoming storms and challenges.

MAN AND not "versus" WOMAN

If the plant or the soil works against each other no one wins. Both lose life and produce little. When they work together, they benefit from each others' traits. Strong plants with strong soil survive even the toughest of winters because of the bonding between them. When it becomes a matter of having to win the disagreement, instead of reaching a compromise, or being "right" as opposed to admitting error, the elements work against each other. In this case, not only can neither the plant nor the soil survive together, but everything in its vicinity suffers as well. The plant and the soil damage the blossoms, seeding or fruit that could have flourished in a harmonized nurturing environment. These damaged blossoms, seeding and fruit become damaged children.

THIRD PARTY FERTILITZATION

An affair outside of one's marriage, taking another partner, or having a focus more important than the committed relationship is comparable to a hand yanking a plant from the ground or a dog urinating on a flower bed. The act is deadly to the plant and soil: the rooted relationship. Being the offender is being the untrained dog. The act of infidelity uproots the natural progressive growth between the plant and the soil. These unnatural interactions deter growth. Natural deterrents are illness and death that can be compared to a hurricane or flood. The hurricane or flood that may challenge the connection of the relationship is an unavoidable cosmic event. These natural interactions are normally expected, accepted and often weathered.

BONUS COMMON SENSE THOUGHT PROCESS:

• If a relationship is not working, there are two acceptable options: work at it or get out of it. Murder is not an acceptable option.

• People who love and are dedicated to their partners will work at the relationship. It takes both to feel both.

• People who do not love and are not dedicated to their partners will hurt, degrade, lie, cheat, wound, and possibly kill.

• The latter type of people define the core of a bad relationship.

• If in a bad relationship, get out before your spirit or you are killed.

WO- AND MEN- NERS

Someone has fallen down on the job, and the injured are not receiving worker's compensation. I know that most of our mothers and fathers told us what was acceptable and what was not. So why are there so many young people who seem totally oblivious to certain manners and unacceptable mannerisms? More pondering is why some adults do not seem to know any better or move to re-educate.

COUGHING, SNEEZING and BODY FLUIDS

When we choose to kiss someone, especially French kiss, we willingly accept to swap fluids with the person. This I accept because I have the choice. I do not accept people who neglect to cover their mouth when they cough or sneeze. I have not agreed to share those fluids, especially those unhealthy and obviously infectious fluids. These same people are so generous with their germs that they want to touch as many items as possible with the same hand that they have wiped their snotty noses. Moreover, they follow through with shaking hands and doing high fives to transfer more of their fluids. There is a new study that promotes sneezing and coughing into the arm. Why not retrain on washing the hands or keeping the antiseptic gels at hand? Literally.

Colds and flu's do not discriminate. Though I am against discrimination, here is one area where I would condone it, wholeheartedly. There is nothing more hygienic than washing your hands. There is nothing more unhygienic than not washing your hands. It is a basic lesson growing up. Today, there are gels to kill bacteria when soap and water are not available. There is no excuse for not being prepared to assist in the prevention of spreading germs. Some people honestly believe that they do not have to wash their hands after using the toilet because they "don't touch anything." Germs are invisible. They can not be seen, yet they are touched and transported. By the time our hands make it to the sink to be washed, the germs have already traveled half the way up the arm, maybe further. I overheard a mother tell her young son that he only had to wash his left hand. Afterwards, they entered the resort's restaurant from the restroom. Wash your hands: both of them. Please.

Ever been on a date and the date returns from the restroom and takes your hand? If their hand is not moist, cold, or clammy, they have not washed their hands. They have just transferred their germs and all the germs of the restroom. They are unclean. Furthermore, they are sharing those germs with you and your dinner.

Though I could have included the art of aiming in urination in the section on "Cleanliness," I wanted to highlight it here. Public toilets are just that: there for the public, thus everyone. Concluding, other persons other than ourselves will need the facility's use. It is our attention and use of good manners that should remind us to leave a clean stall on our departure. Our habits should be to always flush the toilet, so that the next person does not have to be subject to our waste: scent or otherwise. More so, should we miss the seat, we should clean it off. Even if these seats are not sat on, one should not have to fear being subjected to someone else's personal waste. There are times when the hover position over the toilet seat fails. We slip. Finally, please wash your hands before exiting the facility. Habitually some "forget" to wash their hands and others are forced to find ways not to touch the doorknob to make an exit.

YAWNING

Like chewing food with the mouth closed, yawning is accompanied with a hand covering the opening of the mouth. Yawning is one of those body functions that both humans and animals perform. What separates us from animals is the use of good manners. No one but medical professionals should be exposed to the back of the throat. Politeness is explained in our youth along with do not embarrass your parents in public. There are numerous ways to disguise a yawn. Being publicly visible or in a meeting, I suggest the most discreet method as possible to disguise a yawn such as suppressing the yawn by pressing the bottom and top lips closed. Otherwise, simply place one hand in front of the mouth until the yawn is over. I repeat: until the yawn is over.

PLEASE AND THANK Qs

A European once told me that Americans say "Please" and "Thank You" too much. My reply is that they probably do not say it enough. There is nothing wrong with being too polite. Thank You.

There are some people that seem to forget their manners when they are being serviced. Paying for service does not give exclusion from using the "nice" words. Want to order a cocktail from the bartender, want to see an item from a clerk, or need a blanket from the flight attendant: use the words please and thank you. If these "nice words" are not used, do not be surprised when that person does not serve and stares expectedly waiting for the "magic word."

Moreover, there is a difference between when to use "Thank You" and when to use "No, Thank You." As a child, my mother was constantly correcting me when I just said "No" instead of "No, Thank You." The repetition in correction was because she misunderstood that my misuse was not intentional. The difference in when one is proper over the other was not explained. It was assumed. In the service industries, personnel are trained never to say "no." It is explained that the use of the word "no" is followed by childhood flashback responses of the slap on the hand. To say "No" is a "No-No." Negative response answers are therefore longer and more winded to make the "nay" easily accepted.

The proper use of "No, Thank You" is whenever there is an offer that you wish to refuse. I was so well trained by my mother that in the beginning of my resort career a couple invited me to join them: sexually. My quick response was "No, Thank You." As embarrassed as I was, I was at least polite.

JUST SCRATCHING THE SURFACE

I am a woman. I have no balls. Some of my friends would probably disagree. I do not understand that the penis needs to be adjusted to the left or the right or that the testicles can become sweaty and itchy. I do understand that not all men have the need to grab, scratch, or rearrange their lower gems in public view. Thus, I have deduced that having to touch them in public is a conscious decision to ignore having good manners. I am in no way interested in a man who has sweaty balls any more than he should be interested if I had a sweaty, itchy crotch.

Women have something that we do not display a need to relieve in public company. We sometimes have itchy nipples. Ever see any ladies around the world scratching their breast in public? It would be bad manners, even if a turn-on.

74

A side message to men:
Grabbing your crotch to get women to look there is unnecessary. We have already checked it out.

EATING

From scratching the crotch to eating, granted a hard "segway," yet a public function. We can prevent persons eating with their mouth open or hearing persons smacking their lips when they eat. Teach children, friends, mates how to eat. If I decide what I want to eat from the menu, I want to see it on my plate, not in someone's mouth. It is not extremely difficult to close the mouth and chew. If chewing is audible, more than likely the mouth is not closed. Not only is it not polite, but it kills an appetite. Sea food is good, as to see food is not good. Also, do not forget the rule, do not talk with food in the mouth; if chewing and talking at the same time, the mouth is not closed.

In many Asian countries and Asian cultures, it is a compliment to the host to slurp, smack, and make noise when eating. My book is not addressing that culture. When opening the mouth to take another bite, it should not sound like the blowing of wet kisses to an infant. It should not sound like an animal slurping up slop. It should not sound at all.

Of course, I will make exceptions. I hear some of those questions forming in your minds. It is hard to avoid making sounds even with a closed mouth when eating lettuce, cucumbers, nuts, popcorn, crackers, potato chips, or biting into hard candy, and the like. However, the sounds can be minimized by closing the mouth when eating them. As for chewing gum, it is to make breath fresh and the new and improved gum is for whitening a smile. The snap, crackle, and pop sounds are for a certain cereal and not chewing gum.

JUST BETWEEN YOU AND YOU

Do not eat or chew gum while talking on the phone. This sound is similar to nails on a blackboard: unnecessary and equally irritating. The magnified sound coming through the receiver is reaching directly from the mouth into someone else's ear stronger than the offender can detect.

BONUS COMMON SENSE THOUGHT PROCESS:

• Using good manners maintains a polite existence between parties.

• A tense situation can become manageable with the use of good manners.

• A tense situation can become tenser and less manageable with the use of bad manners or no manners at all.

• Using good manners as a habit can help diffuse tense situations.

Get Some – Training in Common Sense

PORT-A-TALK EDIQUETTE

Ringing phones are on the top of my lists of daily irritants. After littering, I find ringing phones unnerving. I am a mobile phone rebel. I am a phone rebel. When one works in a department that has constant phone ringing, and where the company's mobile phone rings only when there is a problem, the lesson learned is to detest the ring of a phone. Even a cute ring tone is annoying to me. When did it become so important that someone reach me whenever and wherever I am? When they connect, they ask, "What are you doing?" Why do they need to know? True, phone ringing sets off anxiety within me, and it is a personal hang-up (pun intended.) I am all for having mobile phones for emergencies. Wasn't this the intent? Is calling me to tell me what a co-worker just did important? Can it not wait until I get home? Better yet, send me an email, but not a text message. Are people afraid to wait to tell something later, so they call immediately? Didn't they ever hear that phrase, "If you forgot, it wasn't important?"

My real annoyance comes from listening to all the different conversations in the world. First, people talk too loud when they are on the phone. Just as we explain the inside voice and the outside voice, someone needs to explain the phone voice. Secondly, some conversations need to wait until they are not in earshot of other people. Not everyone wants to know what Candy did at the Christmas party and worse, I might know Candy...or her husband. In fact, I do not want to know why Junior did not make the senior varsity squad, why the proctologist says it is necessary to add more fiber to a diet, why hair color is not what was anticipated, nor why jealousy emerges because the ex-husband is dating someone younger and prettier. I remember when all this was private business and behind closed doors. I recall when it was not possible to hear a telephone private or business conversation from my seat on an airplane.

Speaking of business, someone must be making a lot of money from all the information that can be profited by being in earshot of some phone calls. I have heard business deals, upcoming meeting information, what the next step is after subject has just exited a meeting, and even when someone is going to be downsized. Less confidential is that when these subjects answer their phones, they give their entire name. In the day and age of Internet searching, it is not hard to trace and not hard to profit from the information put in the airway. Imagine an amateur detective that follows an investment executive, or executive assistant. The average person does not know or acknowledge that they are being followed. The executive assistant is constantly receiving phone calls. Just in taking notes from the conversations overheard, the amateur might be able to know what stock to invest or divest, when the executive is going on vacation, and/or what is their favorite restaurant. Detective work could not be simpler.

BRINGING IT HOME

A home invader could follow his victim and know what time he or she will be getting home, know what they are doing for the evening or weekend, know who is in the house, and know when the home will be vacant just by listening in on a phone conversation.

That is a scary light bulb being lit.
Thus, using a "phone voice" would not only possibly save a life or personal valuables, but also save me from a lot of anxiety.

BONUS COMMON SENSE THOUGHT PROCESS:

• Phone conversations were once confined to chosen personal spaces: homes, offices, and public telephone booths.

• When speaking on public phones, people were aware and wary of other people in earshot.

• With affordable mobile phones, technology has expanded our phone conversations to more public areas.

• As mobile phones became smaller, our voices became larger.

• Using mobile phones in public areas make conversations public.

• The public can hear everything that is being said.

• The public is everyone.

• If you do not want everyone to know yours or other individuals' private business, do not talk about them on mobile phones in public.

Get Some – Training in Common Sense

TRANSIT VIALS and RAIS'N RELATIONS

There is nothing more embarrassing than being an American outside of the United States while other Americans display the personality of what all other nations consider as " the loud, obnoxious American." Even Americans say it about New Yorkers. Even New Yorkers say it about New Yorkers. That is not to say that it is only New Yorkers, but as a nation, we follow the false belief: the bigger, the better. Unfortunately, often this concept includes noise.

Modifying the image is in the training. As a child, I was taught to behave in public, not "act up," and not to embarrass my parents. As adults, we should continue with these concepts: behave in public, not "act up," and not to embarrass our country. Take the example of the United States Olympic Basketball's "Dream Team." They were criticized for not being the proper images that the United States Olympic Committee wanted representing the United States of America internationally, winning or not. This is proof that grabbing the crotch is not acceptable. Imagine the embarrassment that could have been avoided through "Train and Explain" before sending the team abroad. Clear hindsight can be avoided with trained foresight.

As far as being loud Americans, it is our own fault. We forget about our inside voices and our outside voices. Only this time, there is a slight reversal, please modify your inside American voice to an outside American voice when traveling. Teach children the same.

Speaking of children, why does it take the person seated ahead of a child on an airplane to ask the child to stop kicking the seat? Who should get the reprimand: parent or child? Why is the child kicking the seat or playing with the seat tray? It is because he or she is bored. Why is the child bored? It is as a result of Mommy and/or Daddy not preparing before traveling to keep the child occupied and entertained.

Get Some – Training in Common Sense

My mother is a master at teaching people to read, literally. One of her methods to encourage reading is suggesting that children read about subjects they enjoy or have an interest. My mother, a reading specialist, would find out what a child's likes and interests were and find books for that child within their interests. What better way to become entertained and learn at the same time? At an airport, I once heard a young child ask for her book. The mother said no. She would not give the child the book. I was appalled. Denying a child a book seemed not only cruel, but backwards. The result was that the child annoyed everyone else in the waiting area instead of sitting quietly with the book.

A child in comparison to an adult needs more stimulation to stay occupied. Adults need to prepare through time management and organization to keep a child occupied during a trip. A trip could be by plane, car, or another form of transportation. A trip includes short or long distance travel. Included is a routine trip such as one to the doctor's office. In addition, children are always hungry because they are continually burning calories. Their expended energy needs to be fed with more nourishment. If leaving at 5a.m. for the airport, prepare breakfast for the child ahead of time. In these cases, one could prepare a light breakfast the night before the departure. Preparing a snack for the child that can travel is a must. Finally, when arriving at a destination anywhere between 11a.m. and 1p.m., a lunch plan should be prepared in advance. Do not blame the people at the destination for not having food available. Knowledge and preparation are the parent's responsibility.

PLANES

Planes are curious vehicles for children, especially if it is their first time on one. There are so many different buttons and unexplored places that are just calling out to them. Adults do not hear the voices, but the children hear the beckoning loud and clear. We must block out these tempters with our own reasoning. Do not kill the curiosity because that stunts learning. We must train and explain.

The temptation to touch comes from wanting to know what mechanics are behind the control. The constant question "Why?" comes from their curiosity and desire to know more. Before boarding a plane, explain to a child that they will see some things that are off limits. Some of those items may be off limits because they are dangerous (like fire) and some items are off limits because they are not toys. When boarding the plane, show and explain what is allowed and what is not. Show how everything works, so that the curiosity is satisfied. Now, place something new that they *can* touch in front of them: a puzzle, a new book of interest, a challenging word game. There is now something new for the child to occupy their curiosity. The mystery of the plane has already been conquered. Best of all, my seat is not being kicked. Thank You.

Should a child be allowed to walk up and down the plane's aisles? Yes, by all means, but at an appropriate time and with a parent directly behind. It is hard enough for adults to sit still on a plane, imagine how hard it is for children whose entire purpose in life is to play and run around. In addition, roaming the aisle will make them less curious and probably more tired. When not to go like the buffalo roam? Anytime the flight attendants are working the aisles, anytime the seat belt sign is illuminated, and when the child has a dirty diaper. Please and Thank You.

Flying sometimes causes ear discomfort. Most adults know how to regulate the discomfort. Children not only do not know how to regulate it, but they also do not know how they can prepare against it. The mechanics of the ear and how air travel is related can be explained before traveling. The adult needs to prepare with items that will assist the child to experience the least amount of discomfort as possible: pacifier, gum, hard candy, or a nipple. Make sure the airline carrier does not have a policy against breast feeding. Though some may scream this is common sense: some children are too old to be breast fed. If a child can reach for the nipple, pull it out of a blouse, and suckle, that child should have graduated to a bottle or "sippy" cup long ago.

Reaching for something pacifying is not reserved for the children on the flight. Adult travelers need to prepare for their own discomforts. For instance complaining about the child that cries the entire flight accomplishes nothing. Adult travelers know before they get on an airplane that they are sensitive to noise. The noise can be the talking of the people in front, beside, or behind. The noise can be the four-year-old little girl who will not stop asking question to her mother or father. The noise might be another traveler on the flight that has fallen asleep and has a loud snoring symphony playing from his throat. Regardless of the noise, the adult who knows that all of these possibilities are annoying needs to prepare for them before travel. Thus, it is a good investment to buy noise reduction earphones. Their purchase is not only preparation for more individual comfort, but also a comfort for friends who would have to listen to any complaints after the flight.

Get Some – Training in Common Sense

Prior to traveling, there is a concept called: research. If it is a first trip to a destination, research it. Researching has never been so easy. All one has to do is log on to any search engine on the Internet. No longer is there a need to go to an agency or the library, just sit down and type a question and the answers appear in many sites and many opinions. Imagine how prepared and informed some people could be and how they would no longer utter the words, "I didn't know." People who utter the "I did not know" phrase have chosen not to know. Do not blame someone for not giving all the information. Find all the information, ask the correct questions, and be aware.

Before I could ask what a word's meaning was or how a word was spelled, my parents required that I attempt to find the answer. I was trained to "look it up." If I had trouble finding the answer, my parents would assist me in the research. Rarely was the answer just fed to me. As such, I have a hunger for knowledge. Thus, my parents not only "trained and explained," but they taught me how to "train and explain" myself.

BONUS COMMON SENSE THOUGHT PROCESS:

• Misbehaving children are disruptive.

• Disruptive behavior is annoying.

• People who are annoyed with disruptive behaving children are not annoyed with the children.

• People who are annoyed with disruptive behaving children are annoyed with their non-reactive parents.

2 C OR NOT 2 C, NOT A QUESTION

My father, a trial lawyer, used to play observation exercises with me as a child. I thought we were simply playing games. He was preparing me for life and some of its challenges. My belief is this emerged from his annoyances with witnesses during courtroom trials. He had encountered too many witnesses who could not recall what they had seen or heard. He would drive with me as a passenger, and he would ask me how many people were standing on the corner two blocks prior. He would ask me, what color was the car and how many people were in the car that was beside us at the last red light. Little girls never want to disappoint their fathers. The skills honed by these exercises continue in my head long after my father stopped playing them with me.

Being aware of surroundings could save lives. Train and explain why it is important to know where the exits are when entering a place. It is invaluable to know what is where, who is who, and who is where. We do not have the gift of having eyes behind our backs, but we have other body mechanics that help us *feel* our surroundings. We can turn our heads. We can listen with our ears. An amazing trait is that we can digest all of our surroundings in seconds with our minds when previously trained. With training, we can evaluate the situation and deduce why the hairs on the back of our necks rose.

My parents were apt at verifying that their three daughters displayed these skills in every aspect of our lives. My eldest sister, Sheryl, can immediately tell when any item in a room or on her office desk is out of place. My middle sister, Sharon, can get your from point "A" to point "B" with accurate direction, including mileage, and landmarks. I, the youngest, never forget a face.

Many people become victims because they do not listen to their inner voice. The inner voice is the brain analyzing everything the senses have experienced and deducing from it. A person that ignores the inner voice is rejecting reason. There is no reason to reject reason whether understanding the mechanics of it or not. Digest and retain this knowledge and be aware.

Get Some – Training in Common Sense

My parents taught us also not to take unnecessary risks. Safety was not only a way of life, in our household it was one of the rules. Should one wonder why some children are sometime abducted? It is because many were not taught or did not heed the teaching of safety. I was not allowed to enter anyone's house in the neighborhood except my aunts' houses. Sure, friends could come into our house and did. I was strictly forbidden from talking to strangers, accepting anything from anyone I did not know, or getting in or stopping near a strange car. When I received my first bicycle, I could only ride it up and down the pavement of the same side as our house. Imagine my glee when I got to ride it around the block, but I was safe.

The training started at home. The training started before I could leave the house alone. For many years, I was allowed outside, but not off the outside steps of our home. With the training, I was taught the obedience to follow my parents' rules. The fear of what could happen was lesson enough. It was not the fear of my parents. It was the stories that they told to explain why these rules were in place. Today, I can say that their rules kept me safe and to this day: alive.

BONUS COMMON SENSE THOUGHT PROCESS:

• It is late at night and you are walking down a well-lit, well-populated area.

• Safety is in numbers, visibility, and witnesses.

• You are headed back to where you parked your car.

• You have an option to take an approaching side street that will get you to your car faster.

• The side street is neither well-lit nor well-populated.

• You decide to take the side street because you are getting tired and want to get home, maybe beat the traffic.

• You just put your life and anything you value at risk.

• If anyone wants what you have, more than likely, they will be waiting for you on the side street, not where they can be identified or stopped from getting what they want: your money, your things, your virtue, and/or your life.

BURNING YOUR BRITCHES

Sun tanning is a great subject coming from an African American lady such as myself. I do not go out to the beach or pool to tan. I actually like my coloring and complexion. Sometimes, emerging a different shade is unavoidable when protection from the rays is limited. I like outside sports. I like being outside. I was informed at an early age the importance of sun block. Notice that I did not write "oil." People who are still applying oil to their skin and going out in the sun need to refer back to the first chapter on raising children. Please reread the section on fire, burning, and pain.

More importantly, sun exposure is a health risk. Going out in the sun and not protecting the skin is a form of self-abuse and self-neglect. Purposely exposing the skin to the sun, toasting one side for twenty minutes and the other side for twenty minutes (you know who you are) is like roasting a frozen Thanksgiving turkey. Everybody loves the crispy skin, yet few know it is the least healthy of the bird. In fact, those that believe that the red skin will turn brown "after awhile," misconceive what is actually happening. I invite these believers to cook a steak to rare or medium rare and let it sit out for "awhile." Once the red part turns brown, the steak is not fit for consumption; the meat is rotting. Red burned human skin turns brown when the skin cells are dying.

It is not just enough to apply sun block. Reading the instructions on the bottle is a must. Most instructions state that sun block must be applied twenty minutes before sun exposure, liberally, and often. Surprised? Those directions have always been on the bottles. Waiting until clothes have been peeled off, the towel placed, and the lounge chair arranged just so, before applying sun block is a long time unprotected from the harmful rays. Realize that sun block is a chemical element that needs to interact with the body's own chemical structure. It is not comparable to a protective piece of clothing; it is a chemical in liquid or gel form that helps the body to protect itself from the sun's rays when applied and reapplied correctly. If sun block is not applied, the skin will burn.

BONUS COMMON SENSE THOUGHT PROCESS:

• Fire burns.

• The sun is a gigantic ball of fire.

• The sun will burn human skin even when it's covered by clouds.

• Clouds are not a form of sun block.

• Without the use of sun protection, the human skin will hurt; that is why it is call a sun *burn*.

• Having a sunburn is publicly declaring that you lack common sense.

.

TO RODE A GAIN

While living in Florida, some drivers annoy the "bejesus" out of me and it is not because of age. I want to take out bulletin boards all around their state with flashing lights. Hello Floridian, there is a contraption on the car, usually near the steering wheel that when flipped up or down indicates to everyone: drivers in front, drivers in back, drivers to the left, drivers to the right, walkers, bikers, skateboarders, in-line skaters, the seeing eye dog, and whomever else is on the road, street, and sidewalk that the driver is going to turn. This is in class 101 of driving. It is not to be ignored. Using a turn signal is courteous in driving and what is called defensive driving. It prevents accidents. Aggressive driving creates accidents. Think of defensive driving as putting a condom on a car.   Every time a turn is signaled, the act is to protect the car from the act of penetration.

Why do people talk to people in other cars as if they can not be heard? Why do drivers let other drivers aggravate them? Being in a rush, does not mean everyone is in a rush. Calm down and take a deep breath. The person in front may not have the same driving skills but it does not mean they are a "dumb driver." They may be an untrained driver. Yelling, motioning, and moody gazes are not going to train them. If another driver is creating challenges, get out of the way and change the lane. Everyone benefits because everyone is less annoyed, including the other people in the cars.

There is such a practice as driver's etiquette. When someone permits a merge into a lane, wave a hand at the same level as the rearview mirror. This is a gesture of thanks. By exhibiting these manners, the polite driver will not feel slighted.

For those that speed excessively, slow down: death comes soon enough without the use of a metal coffin on wheels.

THINGS NEVER TO DO or TO DO IN THE CAR
(Or any vehicle such as a taxi, bus, or train)

1. Stop picking your nose and cleaning your ears with your finger or the caps and ends of pens; stop picking your teeth or flossing in public. Consider where the waste that emerges becomes deposited.

2. Using mobile phones, putting on make-up, eating meals, and any other distraction is not to be done at the same time as driving.

3. If the car smells, clean it. Those fresheners hanging from the rearview mirror are tacky. They are only disguising the actual problem; the car is dirty or the athletic bag should have been placed in the trunk.

BONUS COMMON SENSE THOUGHT PROCESS:

• Cars are powerful vehicles.

• The misuse of powerful vehicles equals the use of a deadly force.

• Using a deadly force improperly can cause death, intentional or unintentional.

• The use of a deadly force can result in imprisonment.

• Drinking and driving is using an object of deadly force irresponsibly.

• Drinking and driving can kill.

• If someone is killed due to drinking and driving, the result can be imprisonment.

• Unless a masochist who likes to be imprisoned, do not drive if going out drinking.

• Do not get in a car with a masochist or killer.

FEE-FI-FONANCE

STUDENT LOANS

Student loans are a great idea. This is what the average needy students understand, *"The government is giving me money for school because Mom and Dad can not. This is a loan to my parents."* Teenagers do not understand the words "loan" or "payback" unless they have been trained. They understand that they are receiving a gift of money. They have been trained to receive money gifts not money loans with birthday and holiday cards. It is a present. They do not expect to have to pay it back. They have never paid anyone back in their life unless they have been trained. If anything is understood about paying loans back, it is that it is something Moms and Dads do. That is part of the child/parent relationship. Some of these same children get credit cards and mobile phones from Mom and Dad, and they expect that Mom and Dad will pay off the bills. They grow up believing that someone else will pay their debts. A young adult growing into responsibility outside the home hears and understands because of lack of training: *the government is going to give me money to go to college and graduate school. The government will not ask for payback. The government will defer payment* (but they really do not understand this word.) *The payments will start when I am finished school. Mom and Dad will be able to pay the loan. All the money I will earn after and because of my education is mine.*

How can we expect children, teenagers, and later adults to understand the workings of loans and credit cards if they have not experienced the responsibilities behind them. They can not understand 'paying back' if they have never experienced repaying anyone or any company. The concepts behind "credit" need to be taught and explained as they are children. As a result, they will be responsible and reliable credit risks. Promote the little jobs that teach children the importance of finances. Advance money to them and put them on a schedule to repay the loan.

I believe that a psychological and maturity evaluation should be done before giving students loans. It should be determined what the career choices are and if in fact that student is sufficiently ambitious to in the future earn money and repay the good old United States of America. I will call this "Student Risk Management." A rating system should follow. If a student's "Student Risk Management Level (SRML)" falls below a seven, they do not qualify for the loan. The rating is based on the student, not the student's parents. Who rates below a seven? Any student that has not chosen a career path, i.e.: "major" by entry into university/college level. Who rates above: pre-law, pre-med, engineers, economists (who should rate a ten if they have exceptional academic scores), and technology science majors. Everyone, however, should be able to go to university/college whether they can afford it or not.

We have government sponsored public schools. Why do we not have more reputable government sponsored universities? There are not enough State sponsored universities that carry the influence equal to Ivy League universities/colleges. We give more money to non-American poverty, rebuilding, revolutionary, democratic, emerging democratic and corrupt countries every year. Why do we not invest more in American education?

The more of our own we educate, the more prosperous our country becomes. With all their knowledge, more of those college graduates will be able to afford a living.

Get Some – Training in Common Sense

There could be less welfare participants. Here is a concept: maybe we could fade out welfare programs altogether with improved education. Not the first time it has been mentioned and certainly not the last. We need to educate students to succeed and not just "make the grade" with their lessons. Educate: a concept where students leave school able to read, write, spell without spell check, and divide the percentage of an amortization schedule with their salary. How about: Motivate to Graduate and Graduate the Motivated. I will never forget when I was knee high and a strange woman ran up to my mother on a Philadelphia street crying to her and saying, "Thank you, Mrs. Johnson, for teaching me to read. You changed my life." That crazy educated lady looked down at me and told me that my mother was invaluable, beyond human, and indispensable. Not in those exact words, but that is what I understood. My mother is important. My mother is a celebrity among innumerable former students because of her dedication to diminishing illiteracy.

Once we have *weaned* students through college and given them an upper level education, they should understand what a loan is and actually want to pay it back. They have been trained in not only taking but giving back. These students can find jobs, become successful professionals, and prosper. Hopefully, they will train and explain how they have benefited to others.

108

SAVING MONEY

When I was a little girl, my parents opened bank accounts for my sisters and me. It was our responsibility to go and ask our father for $20 each week and go directly to the bank and deposit it in a savings account in our names. I did not know how this money would be used in the future, but I knew it was going to be used for me. This was motivation enough. Every week, I would wait in the waiting room of my father's law firm until he could see me. We would talk like I was there just to say hello on my way home from school. I would ask him for $20 and he would ask "Why do you need $20?" I would answer "…to put in the bank, Daddy." That proceeded for years until my parents built the family a new house. The accounts were cleared out for the purchase. We had to sign forms that gave our parents the permission to withdraw the funds.

I actually thought that I was loaning my parents the money. I always thought that my parents would pay me back. I was a child. I thought that they would reopen those bank accounts and bring the balances back. After all, wasn't that money for me? Wasn't it for my future? As I said, I was a child.

I learned two lessons: First, save money until I find something I want to buy with it. Depending on how much I want to spend in my future, that is how much money and how much time I need to leave it somewhere safe. Banks, safety deposit boxes, or stuffed in the old couch are all popular places to safeguard money, but not wise choices. Second, I do not have to pay back family.

I know that was not the training that I should have received. These lessons were not the training I can use to teach me about building my portfolio. Thus, I am still being trained.

SAVE YOU MUST

Living must be within one's means. If the money is saved for a purchase, whether it is a house or a diamond ring, it will be treasured. If self bought, the purchase will be appreciated and taken care of with vigor. If acquired alone, there will be pride in its ownership. Buying wisely will deter regret in purchases. Wiser purchases will appreciate instead of depreciate. When spending what has been saved, make sure big purchases will ultimately earn more money or give irreplaceable pleasure.

STOCK MARKET

I will admit it. I do not know a thing about this area. EXCEPT, there is money to be made by letting corporations use your money. Investing in their potential to make more money and be successful, pays with earning more than was invested.

I think Ameritrade had the best example with a commercial airing in the winter of 2005. A teenage girl asks her dad for money to buy a pair of jeans. He asks her if they are popular.
Yes, of course, all the kids are wearing them. So with his daughter next to him, he logs onto the Internet, researches the jean company's name brand. Next, father and daughter log onto Ameritrade.com and invest in the brand. It was "Train and Explain" in a TV commercial.

How often has these thoughts passed?
    I should have invested in that?
        Yahoo, Google, TiVo, Dow/Jones, etc
    Why didn't you?
    Who was stopping you?

Only you stopped yourself from listening to your inner reasoning.

CREDIT CARDS

Who are the wicked people that target colleges' and universities' students and encourage the students to open credit accounts? This business is cruel and possibly inhuman. This practice can be compared to loan sharks giving money that they know can not be repaid. Later, they will come to collect, but the students are not earning a living, therefore, the students can not pay. Most students are still relying on Mom and Dad. In gaining credit accounts, many students find themselves in debt with bad credit ratings before entering the job market. These students are in debt before they understand what being "in debt" means.

Adults who have more than one credit card should ask themselves why. Maybe having more than one credit card is too needy. Possibly, there is one credit card for general use and the other for emergencies. Define an emergency and be bound to the definition. Is it when the other credit card does not work? It should not be. I hate it when my credit card gets declined and the merchant asks me, "Do you have another credit card?" I want to answer, "No I don't so please put this back on the shelf because I obviously can not afford it." Actually, I knew I could not afford it, which is why I tried to use the credit card.

112

Get Some – Training in Common Sense

A revolutionary concept: do not obtain or own more than one credit card. The banks and creditors want to silence me for writing this. Instead, use cash or debit cards. Use one credit card *and only one* credit card as an emergency card. If a purchase can not be afforded, do not buy it. The desire to want it "now" is not considered an emergency and will pass. Learn to save for it and deserve it. Fight the impulse to buy now, and later realize that it was not needed after all.

If a full debt on a credit card can not be paid, pay half. Other bills, houses and cars should not be paid with credit cards. Before canceling credit cards, check and negotiate for the best interest rate and keep that account open. When canceling a credit card account, the balance must be zero and instruct the credit company to report that the account was closed by customer request. Furthermore, stop complaining when there are bills to be paid. The bills were created and not miraculously. Now, sit down and pay them, unless Mom and Dad will pay them for you.

Speaking of bills, who in their right mind spends $800 on mobile phone calls? Here is a thought, stop talking on the mobile phone, use a land line, and invest the money saved. Invest in the mobile phone companies; they are showing incredible profits.

BONUS COMMON SENSE THOUGHT PROCESS:

• A penny saved is a penny saved.

• Savings accounts do not promote significant earnings on the penny.

• Wise investments promote earnings on the penny.

• A penny invested can become more than a few pennies.

• Invest the pennies.

"GOD BLESS THE CHIL' THAT'S GOT HIS OWN"

DO WHAT YOU KNOW AND DO IT WELL

Excerpts of the lyrics written by Billy Holiday and Arthur Herzog, Jr. are "Papa may have and Momma may have, but GOD bless the child that's got his own."

Claim your own gold, make your own money, build your own future, and foremost, love yourself.

Here it is: my final words.

If you do not love yourself, no one will. Stop the self-pity; we are all tired of it. If you want to dive into a funk, enjoy it, but not too long. Do not take other people down with you. Bottom line, get over it. Do what Joan Rivers used to suggest: "Grow Up!"

Disturbing to me is women crying about sexual harassment. If a man fires a sexual comment, fire one back, only make it hurt. If he touches inappropriately, grab his balls….and not like a wimp. Grab those balls so he limps away knowing he better never approach in that way again. Afterwards, take him to court. In one of my resort jobs for three weeks…who knows maybe more, some co-workers thought it was funny to play with my breast. I would politely ask them to stop. They would not. Finally, I was done being polite. When their hands went up for a feel, they cleared a path for my hand. I only needed one hand for one good grab. Guess what? No more trouble…ever. I was empowered for life. We become victims because we let people see us as victims. We become targets because we ignore all the warning signs. We cease to be aware because we choose not to open our eyes. If there are warning signs and they are ignored, it is a conscious choice to ignore them. Choosing to ignore the warnings when there are signs is ignoring the self. Thus the self is not empowered. HELLOOOO! The mind recognizes the "type" of person that is an abuser and a harasser. All the data has been completed and stored from the media and other peoples' experiences. Do not be in the company of a person the brain is screaming warnings of danger. I am not saying that one should not proceed to file suit against anyone that violates or harasses. I am saying there are signs to help us from being a victim that needs to file a suit.

EMPOWERMENT

We are all allowed to be depressed. Emotions are what make us human. The lows make the highs more meaningful, more enjoyable. That is life. Staying in the funk too long is when it is unhealthy. For more on that, see a doctor. Maybe even seek medical treatments. There is nothing wrong with what some medications have to offer. We, each one of us, need to empower ourselves. Learn to love the self including all its shortcomings and faults. No one is perfect. No one human was meant to be.

I once had the worse eczema attack of my life. I was in a part of Pennsylvania that did not believe in conventional medicines. The facial part of the extensive rash prevented me from opening my eyes. My health declined. The rashes covered my body and there were yellow, smelly liquids oozing from dry cracks in my skin. I was the Mohave Desert. As vain as a nineteen-year- old can be, I just wanted to die. Really! According to my fate, I was at the time enrolled in one of my college required Philosophy and Religious Studies courses. We had just read chapters on death and dying. To my surprise, the course's professor: Dr. Puffenberger came to see me in my dorm room. The feelings I had not shared with anyone, he read me in less than a few minutes. He saw right through to my desperate depression. A month after my recovery, to my shock and horror, he brought to light my personal low in front of a classroom of fellow students when we studied the chapter on suicide. Of course my first instinct was to feel embarrassed. I did not, however, feel ashamed. I was empowered. I learned. I had survived. I was stronger for the experience and the pain. Feeling depressed and desperate in my state was normal. Thinking of ending my pain in a final way was normal. Sharing my feelings with others was empowering. I learned that when reaching that lowest low and rising from it: the rest of life is manageable. No experience can take you lower than wanting to kill yourself. I want you to read that again…. No experience can take you lower than wanting to kill yourself. However, after having hit rock bottom and surviving, everything else that life's challenges bring can be conquered. Rise up! Get it. Get empowered. Get some. Get yours. Thank you to the professor that took the time to come to my room. Thank you to the professor that took the time to "train and explain." Thank you to the professor that saved my life and helped me realize my sanity many times over. Thank you to Elisabeth Kübler-Ross who wrote and developed the principles that the professor explained to me.

LASTING WORDS

Depend on self first for everything. Do not seek a man or woman to buy gifts, give love, and provide serenity or security. "...Child," you should "... [Get] Your Own."

Get Some – Training in Common Sense

EPI LOG

No psychology degree, no sociology degree, just a lady sharing some common sense. I hereby award myself with a B.A. in C.S, yes, and maybe a little B.S. I have never had children and during the editing of this book have been informed that I may not bare children. Withstanding not having my own children, I have trained many parents' children. I long ago realized that not everyone was lucky enough to have parents like mine who care about me. I care about people. I think everyone needs to care about each other. I want to share the fortune of knowledge that I inherited. In so many ways, I was and continue to be well trained. Training should never stop. Training and learning is the true relationship commitment defined by until death "we do part." Continuing to learn is a marriage contract that you commit to with yourself.

I do not agree with the phrase credited to E.C. Brewer that "you can not teach an old dog new tricks." Dogs have been doing it in present years when the law mandated poop scooping.

You can believe me and you can choose not to believe. I could be wrong about some things...or everything.... It is not a secret. It wouldn't be uncommon sense.